BAH
MEANS
BUY A
HOUSE

THE ASK ANTWAUN PLAYBOOK
for BUILDING MILITARY WEALTH

LEVERAGE YOUR BENEFITS.
SECURE YOUR FREEDOM. BUILD LEGACY.

ASK ANTWAUN

BAH Means Buy A House
The Ask Antwaun Playbook for
Building Military Wealth

ISBN: 979-8-9936505-0-0

Published by AskAntwaun Media

All inquiries: AskAntwaun@gmail.com
Printed in the United States of America

Book Design by Williams DocuPrep
www.williamsdocuprep.com

Table of Contents

Introduction

My Journey from Military Service to Financial Enlightenment

In April 2000, fresh out of Forest Park High School in Clayton County, Georgia, I signed the dotted line and raised my right hand. At 18, I thought I was just joining the Army to serve my country and find some direction. What I didn't realize was that decision would be the first major investment I ever made in myself.

Thirteen years later, I left the service as a Chief Warrant Officer 2. I had PCS'd five times, deployed twice, and, like most of us, lived that relentless "hurry up and wait" pace that defined military life in the early 2000s. By the time I hung up the uniform in 2013, I'd built a résumé full of achievements but not a lot of wealth.

Even after transitioning to a civilian role with the Department of Defense, I stayed in that same comfort zone of a steady paycheck, decent benefits, and a predictable routine. I thought I was doing alright. But deep down, I knew I was just maintaining, not multiplying. Then came the moment that changed everything.

The Millionaire Couple That Woke Me Up

I'll never forget it. I was a Staff Sergeant at the time. I was about six years in when I came across an article about a military couple who were on track to retire as millionaires. Not because of a lottery win or a side hustle, but from using their military pay the right way. They'd done it through consistent investing, homeownership, and smart use of their benefits. It stopped me cold.

How was that even possible? We had the same jobs, the same pay scale, and the same benefits. I remember looking at my bank account. I had maybe a thousand bucks in savings, if that, and I realized I was missing something big. That day planted the seed that completely changed how I saw money.

From Survival to Strategy

What I eventually learned is that wealth isn't about income, it's about intention. It's not where you start, it's how you move. I used to think the harder I worked, the wealthier I'd become. But working hard doesn't automatically build wealth, working smart does.

Here's the truth that hit me like a brick:

- Poor people spend all their money.
- The middle class save their money.
- The wealthy invest their money.

That's it. That's the difference.

Once I understood that, everything shifted. I started looking at my paycheck, my BAH, my benefits, and my opportunities differently. Instead of asking, "Can I afford this?" I started asking, "How can I make this work for me?" That mindset, that shift, was my financial awakening.

Why I Wrote This Book

This book is for the Soldier, Sailor, Airman, Marine, or guardian who's ever looked at their LES and wondered, "Where does it all go?" It's for the ones who feel stuck between surviving and thriving, who want to take care of their families now but still build something lasting for later. And it's especially for those who don't realize that the benefits you already have are the keys to wealth if you use them right.

You've earned these benefits. You've served, you've sacrificed, you've moved when told, and you've adapted under pressure. The goal now is to make those same skills work for you not just in service, but in wealth-building.

This isn't a get-rich-quick book. It is a get-real-about-your-finances book. I am going to break down what I wish someone had told me 20 years ago. I will teach you how to use your VA loan, your BAH, your PCS moves, your TSP, and even your military mindset to build real wealth, one intentional move at a time.

Golden Nugget Tips

- **Your BAH is not just an allowance, it is leverage.** You can turn it from rent money into wealth by owning instead of renting. BAH means Buy A House.

- **Invest in knowledge before you invest in property.** The right education can save you thousands and make you hundreds of thousands later.

- **Your paycheck isn't your ceiling.** Military benefits from your VA loan to your TSP match are the hidden bonuses most people overlook.

Next Moves

- Take stock of your current financial position. Don't sugarcoat it. Be real.

- Identify one benefit you've been underusing (BAH, VA loan, TSP).

- Commit to learning how to make that benefit work harder for you.

The journey you're about to take through these pages is not theory; it's real, lived experience. I've made the mistakes, so you don't have to. I've learned the lessons, and now I'm paying them forward.

Because remember, knowledge is leverage.

Need real estate answers?

Just Ask Antwaun.

"Want a head start? You don't have to wait until the last page to take action. Scan below to schedule your 1-on-1 Strategy Session with Antwaun Hill, and let's start building your plan while you read."

Chapter 1

Understanding Military Pay: The Foundation of Wealth Building

People join the military for all kinds of reasons: to serve, to travel, to earn money for college, to find direction, or simply to build a more stable life. Whatever the reason, one thing is true: the U.S. military offers one of the most reliable paychecks on the planet.

You might not always love your assignment, but you can count on that deposit hitting on the 1st and the 15th like clockwork. Whether you're the hardest worker in your unit or skating by just enough to stay under the radar, your pay hits on time, every time. That kind of consistency is rare in the civilian world. And let's be honest... getting fired from the military? That's a long, complicated process. Job security doesn't get much stronger than that.

But here's the twist. Stability isn't the same as strategy. Just because you get paid consistently doesn't mean you're building wealth consistently. And that's where understanding your pay, really understanding it, becomes the foundation for everything that follows.

Breaking Down the Military Pay Structure

Your compensation in the military isn't just "a paycheck." It's a system that's designed with multiple parts, each serving a purpose. Once you know how to use each part strategically, you start seeing your income differently. You start seeing leverage.

Basic Pay – The Core

Basic pay is your foundation. It's your base salary and the biggest portion of your income. It's determined by your rank and years of service, and you'll see it deposited twice a month, on the 1st and the 15th. The 1st is your "end-of-month" pay. Don't ask why; just accept that's how it works.

Like any regular paycheck, Basic Pay is taxable. It's predictable, steady, and forms the backbone of your financial planning.

Allowances – The Hidden Advantage

Here's where things get interesting. Allowances are where most service members start to unlock the hidden wealth inside their pay; they just don't realize it.

Allowances are tax-free forms of compensation meant to offset specific living costs. They don't show up on your taxable income, which means they help you take home more money every month without bumping you into a higher tax bracket. The two most common ones are **BAS** and **BAH.**

- **BAS (Basic Allowance for Subsistence)** is meant to cover your meals. It's for *you*, not your family — a nod to the days when the military provided room and board as part of your service.

- **BAH (Basic Allowance for Housing)** helps with housing costs when government quarters aren't available. It varies based on location, pay grade, and whether you have dependents. It's calculated from local rental data, so if you're stationed in Hawaii, California, or D.C., your BAH will be much higher than someone stationed in Kansas or Oklahoma.

And again, both are tax-free. That's free money most people don't realize they're not maximizing.

Other Key Allowances You Might Not Think About

- **COLA (Cost of Living Allowance):** For high-cost duty stations like Hawaii or overseas this helps maintain your purchasing power.

- **DLA (Dislocation Allowance):** Helps cover the costs of moving during a PCS. Think deposits, setup fees, cleaning supplies, and all those "hidden" moving expenses.

- **FSA (Family Separation Allowance):** Compensates for the financial strain when you're involuntarily separated from your dependents for duty.

- **FSSA (Family Supplemental Subsistence Allowance):** For those stationed outside the U.S. with larger families who meet certain income criteria. It's designed to ensure your family doesn't struggle to meet basic needs.

This list isn't exhaustive, but it gives you a picture of how layered your military compensation really is. When you add up the base pay, the allowances, the bonuses, and the benefits, the earning potential over a career is massive.

So if military pay has historically outpaced inflation, why are so many service members still living paycheck to paycheck?

The Real Problem: Financial Literacy

Here's the uncomfortable truth. It's not about how much we make; it's about how we manage it. Military families aren't struggling because of low pay. They're struggling because no one ever taught us how to use that pay strategically.

We know how to read a 9-line medevac or prep a convoy brief, but most of us never learned how to read a pay stub beyond checking that the deposit hit. We see our LES and think, "As long as I'm not in the red, I'm good." But that's not wealth building; that's survival. Financial literacy is the missing piece.

When you understand your pay, you realize the military didn't just give you a job, it gave you a system of financial leverage. The question is, will you use it or waste it?

Golden Nugget Tips

- **Know your LES like you know your MOS.** Don't just glance at it; break it down. Understand what every acronym, deduction, and allowance means. That's your financial report card.

- **Your BAH is your biggest wealth-building tool.** Don't just "spend" it on rent, learn how to own with it. (We'll go deep on that in Chapter 2.)

- **Leverage tax-free pay.** Allowances like BAH and BAS aren't taxed, meaning you can redirect that advantage into savings or investments without losing a dime to Uncle Sam.

Next Moves

- Pull up your latest LES. Highlight every line item you don't fully understand. Look them up or ask someone who knows; even better, **Ask Antwaun**.

- Calculate your total tax-free income each month (BAH, BAS, COLA). That's your real wealth advantage.

- Write down one goal for turning part of your BAH into ownership, even if it's just learning how the VA loan works.

Military pay gives you a foundation, but it's what you build on top that creates freedom. Every dollar has a job. Every benefit has potential. And in the chapters ahead, we're going to unlock every one of them step by step.

Chapter 2

The Power of Savings: Establishing Your Financial Security Net

If there's one thing we all know deep down, it's that we should be saving money. The problem isn't knowing; it's doing. Most of us don't fully understand why saving matters or how powerful it actually is when done with consistency and purpose. For years, I treated saving like something I'd "get to later." The result? Every "later" came with a new emergency, a new bill, or a new reason I couldn't get ahead.

Saving isn't about being frugal; it's about being prepared. It's about buying yourself peace of mind. And for military families, that peace of mind is priceless.

Saving: The Foundation of Financial Readiness

Let's strip it down. Saving simply means putting money aside for future use. But don't think of it as money sitting idle; think of it as a financial safety net that keeps you from falling when life throws punches.

There are two main goals with saving:

1. Cover future expenses.

2. Protect yourself from financial stress.

Savings accounts typically offer low risk and modest returns, meaning your money is safe, even if it's not growing fast. It's not supposed to. Saving is about security, not speed.

Investing, on the other hand, is about growth; it comes with higher risk and higher reward. So here's the difference in simple terms:

- Saving = guaranteed small return (interest).

- Investing = potential higher return (but with possible loss).

Both matter, but saving comes first. You can't invest confidently if you don't have a cushion.

The Three Pillars of Building Wealth

No matter how much money you make, wealth is built on three things:

1. Time

2. Consistency

3. Rate of Return (RoR)

Both saving and investing rely on the first two, but your RoR determines how fast your money grows. Let's break this down.

Time: Your Greatest Financial Weapon

In the military, time in service equals rank, benefits, and experience. In finance, time equals compounding, the secret to building real wealth.

Savings goals fall into three timelines:

- **Emergency (less than 1 year):** Build a cushion of 3–6 months' worth of expenses. It's not just about the amount; it's about forming the habit.

- **Short-Term (1–10 years):** Save for vacations, holidays, PCS costs, or tax payments.

- **Long-Term (10+ years):** Think retirement, kids' education, or homeownership. The longer you give your money to grow, the more it compounds.

Time is the one resource you can't earn back. Start early, stay consistent.

Consistency: The Quiet Power Move

Consistency beats intensity every time. Saving $50 every pay period may not sound like much, but it's life-changing over time.

Let's look at SFC Doe:

He saves $50 from each paycheck for 20 years. That's $24,000 total. But here's where the magic happens with a 3% interest rate, his total grows to $32,830. That extra $8,830 wasn't from working harder; it was from compound growth.

Compound interest means your money earns interest, then that interest earns more interest.

It's the financial version of "set it and forget it."

Rate of Return: The Growth Factor

Your RoR determines how fast your money multiplies. Savings accounts are safe but slow. The national average is around **0.59% APY**. If you want your money to grow faster, you'll need tools that offer higher returns without gambling it all away.

Choosing the Right Place to Save

Different tools serve different purposes. Here's a quick breakdown:

Type	Risk	Liquidity	Typical Use	Return
Savings Account	Very low	High	Emergency fund	Low
Certificate of Deposit (CD)	Low	Low	Medium & long-term goals	Medium & long-term goals
Money Market Account (MMA)	Low, moderate	Moderate	Short-term	Slightly higher

The rule of thumb: the more access (liquidity) you have to your money, the lower your return will be. Savings accounts are perfect for your emergency fund. CDs work for planned goals like a car purchase or moving costs. MMAs balance both higher returns and limited access.

Leveling Up: Turning Savings Into Wealth with the TSP

Once you've built your emergency fund, it's time to move beyond saving and into investing. For service members, that starts with the Thrift Savings Plan (TSP).

Think of the TSP as the military's 401(k). It's a tax-advantaged retirement account that lets you invest part of your paycheck into a mix of funds. You choose whether to contribute before taxes (Traditional TSP) or after taxes (Roth TSP).

If you're under the Blended Retirement System (BRS), here's the breakdown:

- The government automatically contributes 1% of your base pay.

- If you contribute 5%, the government matches it dollar for dollar up to another 4%.

That's free money.

Golden Nugget

Never contribute less than 5%. Anything below that is like turning down a bonus.

How the TSP Builds Wealth

Remember our three pillars: time, consistency, rate of return. The TSP nails all three.

- **Time:** The earlier you start, the longer your money compounds.

- **Consistency:** Contributions come straight out of your paycheck automatic discipline.

- **Rate of Return:** You choose your mix of funds, based on your risk, comfort and goals.

TSP Fund Breakdown (Simplified)

Fund Description Risk Level

Fund	Type of Investment	Description	Risk Level
G Fund	Government securities	Steady, low growth	Very Low
F Fund	Bonds	Moderate growth	Low

C Fund	S&P 500	Strong long-term growth	Moderate
S Fund	Small/mid-cap stocks	Big potential, more risk	High
I Fund	International stocks	Global diversification	High
L Funds	Lifecycle funds	Automatically adjust risk as you near retirement	Variable

If you're young, lean toward growth funds (C, S, I), they'll give you better long-term returns. As you near retirement, you can shift to safer options like G or F to protect your balance.

Why the TSP Outperforms Regular Savings
Let's go back to SFC Doe again.

- **Savings Account:** $50 per paycheck for 20 years at 0.59% = ~**$25,000 total.**
- TSP (7% average return + match): Same $50 per paycheck could grow to $50,000+ or more.

That's double with no extra effort, just smarter placement.

The lesson:
Savings protect you. TSP multiplies you.

You already serve your country; now it's time to make your money serve you. The TSP isn't just a benefit; it's a weapon. Use it early, use it often, and let compounding do the heavy lifting.

Golden Nugget Tips

1. **Save first, invest second.** Build your emergency fund before chasing returns.

- **Contribute at least 5% to your TSP.** That's the threshold for full matching of the free money you've earned.

- **Automate your savings.** The best savers don't rely on willpower; they rely on systems.

Next Moves

- Review your current savings plan. Do you have 3–6 months of expenses saved?

- Open a high-yield savings account for your emergency fund.

- Enroll or log into your TSP account and check your contribution rate; bump it up to at least 5%.

- Learn your TSP fund mix and rebalance annually.

Saving is the first step toward independence. Investing is the next. Together, they create the stability and growth that transform your income into freedom.

Chapter 3

Investing 101: Making Your Money Work for You

You've probably heard someone say, "You need to make your money work harder for you than you work for it." It sounds good, right? But most of us were never taught what that actually means.

Let's fix that.

When you invest, you're not just *saving* money, you're putting your dollars to work. Investing means buying something that has the potential to *grow* in value or *generate income* over time. The most common tools are **stocks**, **bonds**, **mutual funds**, and **ETFs** (exchange-traded funds).

When you invest, you're chasing one of two outcomes:

- **Appreciation** – the value of what you own goes up.

- **Income** – the investment itself pays you without selling it (dividends or interest).

The smartest investors look for both.

How Money Makes Money

There are two main ways your money can earn for you:

1. **Dividends** – These are payments companies make to shareholders from their profits. Mature, stable companies often pay dividends in cash or additional stock.

   Example: You own shares in a company that pays $1 per share annually. If you own 500 shares, you'll earn $500 a year just for holding the stock.

2. **Interest Payments** – These come from lending your money, like with bonds or even savings accounts. In those cases, *you* are the lender, and the borrower pays you interest over time.

That brings us to one of the most powerful financial forces in existence: **interest** and, more specifically, the key difference between *simple* and *compound* interest.

Simple vs. Compound Interest: The $1,000 Difference

Let's use a real-world scenario.

PFC Johns just received a $25,000 enlistment bonus. After taxes, he has $18,000 left and wants to invest it.

Simple Interest: Simple interest earns only on the original amount (principal).

Formula: Principal × Rate × Time

- PFC Johns puts his $18,000 into a 6-year certificate of deposit (CD) at 6%.

- $18,000 × 0.06 × 6 = $6,480

- After six years, his total is $24,480 ($18,000 + $6,480). Not bad for a safe, no-stress option.

Compound Interest

Now let's see what happens with compounding, where your interest earns more interest.

Formula: $P \times (1 + r)^n - P$

- $18,000 \times (1 + .06)^6 - \$18,000 = \$7,533.34$
- Total value: $25,533.34

Same money. Same time. But compound interest earns $1,053 more. That's the difference between *earning money* and *building wealth*.

Golden Nugget
Compound interest is like reinforcements.
Every dollar you save recruits another
dollar to fight for you.

Types of Investments

Here's a quick breakdown of the most common investment types and what they do.

Stocks (Equities)

Buying stock means owning a piece of a company. When that company grows, your piece becomes more valuable, and you may receive dividends.

High reward, but also higher risk. Stocks can fluctuate with the market, so patience is key.

Mutual Funds

These pool money from many investors to buy a diversified mix of stocks and/or bonds. They're managed by professionals, which means convenience, but you'll pay small management fees.

Exchange-Traded Funds (ETFs)

ETFs work like mutual funds but trade like individual stocks on an exchange. They often track an index (like the S&P 500), offer broad diversification, and usually cost less to own.

Each of these offers potential growth, but none are risk-free, which brings us to the next point.

Understanding Risk vs. Reward

Every investment carries risk, the possibility that your money could lose value. But without risk, there's no reward. The goal isn't to avoid risk; it's to manage it.

Two Types of Risk

1. **Systematic Risks** – Market-wide risks that affect everyone.

   - **Interest Rate Risk:** Changes in rates can affect bond values.

   - **Market Risk:** The overall market dips and takes everything with it.

   - **Political Risk:** Instability or government changes can shake markets.

2. **Unsystematic Risks** – Specific to a company or industry.

- **Business Risk:** The company's management or operations fail.

- **Credit Risk:** A bond issuer doesn't pay what's owed.

- **Sector Risk:** A particular industry (like tech or real estate) slumps.

A disciplined investor doesn't panic when markets dip, they diversify, stay consistent, and keep their long game in focus.

Risk vs. Reward: Finding Your Balance

The higher the risk, the greater the potential reward and the greater the potential loss. The key is matching your investment choices to your goals and timeline.

- Short-term goals? Keep it conservative: savings accounts, CDs, or low-risk bonds.

- Long-term goals? Take calculated risks: ETFs, index funds, or diversified stock portfolios.

Remember Don't invest money you can't afford to lose. And don't go it alone if you don't have to. Talk to a trusted advisor or someone who's been there. I'll always tell my clients you can learn this stuff, but you don't have to learn it the hard way.

Golden Nugget Tips
1. **Start early, even if it's small.** Compounding favors time over amount.

2. **Diversify.** Don't put all your money in one company, fund, or sector.

3. **Stay the course.** The market goes up and down; the winners are those who stay consistent through both.

4. **Reinvest your earnings.** Dividends and interest grow fastest when you reinvest them.

Next Moves
- Log in to your TSP or investment app and review your current allocation.

- Start a beginner investment account (like a Roth IRA or brokerage) if you don't have one.

- Set a recurring investment, even $25 per paycheck.

- Learn one new investing concept per month (ETFs, index funds, or compounding).

Investing is how you shift from earning a paycheck to building freedom. It's not about luck, timing, or guessing the next big stock. It's about understanding how money multiplies and positioning yourself to benefit. You've worked hard for your income. Now it's time for your income to work hard for you.

Chapter 4

Real Estate and the VA Loan: Building Wealth Through Homeownership

When most people think of the VA loan, they think "no down payment." That's true, but if that's all you see, you're missing the bigger picture. The VA loan isn't just a benefit. It's a wealth-building weapon. It's the single most powerful financial tool the U.S. military gives its service members, and yet most don't fully use it.

From Renter to Owner — The Mindset Shift

For years, I was like most soldiers: I treated my BAH like bonus money. Every PCS meant another rental. I'd hand over my housing allowance to a landlord, pay the rent on time, and move on when orders dropped. But here's the thing: every one of those landlords was using my BAH to pay off their mortgage. That's when it hit me: If my BAH could buy someone else a house, it could have bought me one too.

That's the entire philosophy behind **BAH Means Buy A House**. Stop thinking of your housing allowance as temporary support and start seeing it as permanent leverage.

Understanding the VA Loan

The VA loan was created in 1944 under the GI Bill to help service members and veterans become homeowners without the usual barriers of civilian lending.

It's a government-backed loan. That means lenders take less risk because the VA guarantees a portion of it. That guarantee is what allows the program's best benefits:

1. **No Down Payment** – You can finance 100% of the home's value.

- **No Private Mortgage Insurance (PMI)** – Civilian loans often charge PMI if you put less than 20% down. VA loans skip it completely.

- **Competitive Interest Rates** – Because of the VA guarantee, lenders offer better rates.

- **Flexible Credit Requirements** – The VA focuses more on your ability to repay than a credit-score cutoff.

- **Assumable Loan** – If you sell later, a qualified buyer (veteran or civilian) can assume your low-rate loan instead of getting a new one.

That last one, *assumability*, is a secret weapon we'll dig into later. But first, let's talk about how the VA loan actually builds wealth.

How Homeownership Builds Wealth

Owning property does three things no rental ever will:

1. **Equity Growth** - Every mortgage payment increases your ownership stake in the home. Instead of paying rent forever, part of each payment comes back to you in the form of equity.

- **Appreciation** - Over time, real estate values tend to rise. Even modest annual growth adds up fast. A $500k home that appreciates 3% a year adds $15k in equity without you doing anything.

- **Tax Advantages** - Homeowners can deduct mortgage interest and property taxes (check current IRS rules). Lower taxes mean more money in your pocket.

Add those together and you realize: every PCS move isn't just a transfer; it's a potential wealth move.

Real Talk: The Cost of Not Owning

Let's break this down. If you pay $3,000 a month in rent for 10 years, you've spent $360,000 and built $0 in equity. If you own a home with a $3,000 monthly mortgage, after 10 years you've paid down principal, gained appreciation, and likely built $150k – $200k+ in equity. That's the difference between *spending* your BAH and *owning* your future.

The VA Loan in Action

Meet Staff Sergeant Ramos. She earns $3,669 BAH and pays $2,200 in rent. After attending a VA loan seminar, she realizes that for the same BAH she could own a $500k home at 3.5% interest with no down payment.

She buys a townhouse near base. Three years later, she PCS's and rents it out. The tenant's rent covers the mortgage, she pockets $300 a month, and she still collects full BAH at her new duty station. That's the power of using benefits strategically.

Common Misconceptions About VA Loans

1. **"It's only for veterans."** False. Active-duty, Guard, and Reserve can qualify too.

- **"I can only use it once."** Wrong. You can use your entitlement again after selling or restoring it.

- **"VA loans take too long to close."** Not true if you work with a VA-experienced agent and lender (wink).

- **"I can't own and PCS."** You can rent your home out and keep building equity while you're gone.

Golden Nugget

The VA loan isn't a one-time ticket, it's a reusable asset that can fund multiple homes throughout your career.

Understanding Entitlement & Limits

Your entitlement is the amount the VA guarantees on your behalf not your loan limit. You can have more than one VA loan if your entitlement and income support it. In high-cost areas (like Hawaii or California), that guarantee can cover homes well above $1 million with no money down. Always verify with a VA-specialized lender before assuming you've "maxed out."

From Homeowner to Investor

The most overlooked benefit of the VA loan is its potential for scaling. You can buy a home with zero down, live in it a year, then PCS and rent it out, turning each assignment into an investment opportunity.

Here's a real example:

- Buy Home #1 at your first duty station using the VA loan.

- PCS a year later, rent it out while you use your remaining entitlement for Home #2.

- Repeat.

By the time you retire, you could own multiple properties, each funded with BAH and backed by the VA loan you earned.

Golden Nugget

Each PCS move can either reset your life or build your legacy. The difference depends on how you choose to use your benefits.

How to Prepare Financially for Homeownership

1. **Know Your Budget.** Before house hunting, calculate your monthly comfort zone based on income and BAH.

2. **Check Your Credit.** VA loans are flexible, but better credit often means better rates.

3. **Get Pre-Approved with a VA Lender.** Not every lender understands VA loans. work with one who does.

4. **Plan for PCS Exit Strategy.** If you might move in 3–5 years, buy a property you could easily rent later.

5. **Save for Closing Costs & Maintenance.** No down payment doesn't mean no costs. Prepare for repairs and fees.

Golden Nugget Tips

1. **Use your BAH as leverage.** Convert it from rent to ownership equity.

- **Don't skip the inspection.** VA loans protect you, but it's still your responsibility to buy wisely.

- **Know your exit strategy before you buy.** Think ahead about whether you'll sell or rent when you PCS.

- **Work with a VA-savvy agent.** Not every realtor understands assumptions, entitlement, and occupancy rules. Find one who does (yes, that's your **Ask Antwaun moment**).

Next Moves

- Check your COE (Certificate of Eligibility) through VA.gov or your lender.

- Calculate your buying power using your BAH and current rates.

- Research the housing market at your duty station. See what ownership could cost versus renting.

- Schedule a consult with a VA-focused agent to map your first purchase plan.

Buying a home is more than a milestone; it's a mission. Your service earned you the right to this benefit; now make sure it serves you back. Use your BAH wisely. Leverage your VA loan strategically. And watch how ownership turns into freedom.

Chapter 5

BAH Means Buy A House: Turning Allowance into Ownership

If you take nothing else from this book, take this: BAH isn't just money to live on; it's leverage to live better. Every month, the government deposits your Basic Allowance for Housing (BAH) like clockwork. You earn it, you spend it, and for most service members, it disappears just as fast. But here's the truth most people never think about: your BAH can buy someone a house so why not let it buy yours? That's the core of what I teach every service member I meet: *BAH Means Buy A House*.

The Hidden Power of BAH

Your BAH isn't "extra pay." It's *tax-free income* meant to cover your housing costs. But instead of treating it like rent money, think of it as your government-backed investment fund.

Here's why:

- It's steady and guaranteed.
- It's tax-free.
- It's sized to your duty station's housing market.

In other words, Uncle Sam is literally paying you to maintain housing and that income can qualify you for a mortgage.

Let's do some quick math:

- If your BAH is $3,000/month, that's **$36,000 per year** of housing income. Over a 3-year tour, that's **$108,000.** Money that either builds *your landlord's equity* or *your own*.
- The question is: whose name will be on the deed?

Why Most Military Families Miss the Opportunity

There are three main reasons service members don't buy:

1. **They think they'll move too soon**. But PCS doesn't have to mean selling. You can rent the property and let it pay for itself.

2. **They think they can't afford it**. With the VA loan, you often don't need a down payment, and your BAH covers the mortgage.

3. **They think it's too complicated**. It's not. You just need the right team (VA lender + VA-savvy agent).

The truth is, every PCS move is a fork in the road: you can reset your life or build your legacy. The ones who build wealth are the ones who *plan ahead*.

The BAH-to-Equity Formula

Let's break down how this actually works.

- Say you're stationed in Hawaii earning $3,669 BAH. You find a home priced at $550,000.

- Using a VA loan at 3.5% interest, your principal and interest payment might be around $2,470/month. Add property taxes, insurance, and HOA fees and you're still under your BAH.

That means the government covers your mortgage *and* your equity growth every month.

Now, fast forward three years:

- You've paid down about $25,000 in principal.

- The home appreciated by 10% (~$55,000).

- You've gained $80,000+ in equity just by using your BAH strategically.

That's how real wealth begins, not by saving scraps, but by leveraging the benefits you already have.

PCS Moves as Wealth Moves

Let's say you PCS to Virginia next.

- Instead of selling your old home, you rent it out for $3,000/month. The rent covers the mortgage, you pocket $200 in cash flow, and the tenant keeps building your equity.

- Then you use your remaining VA entitlement to buy your next home with *no down payment again*.

- Do that 2–3 times across your career, and you'll retire with multiple properties all bought with BAH and PCS orders.

Golden Nugget:
PCS doesn't stand for "Permanent Change of Station"; it stands for "Positioning Cash Smart."

Rent vs. Own: The Real Comparison

Scenario Rent Own (VA Loan)

Category	Renting	Buying
Monthly Payment	$3,000	$3,000
Duration	3 years	3 years
Equity Built	$0	~$80,000
Tax Benefits	None	Mortgage & property deductions
Ownership	Landlord's	Yours
Long-Term Impact	Temporary	Permanent

Key takeaway:

Every dollar of rent is gone forever. Every dollar of a mortgage builds your financial foundation.

Common BAH Pitfalls

Even with the best intentions, here's where service members slip:

1. **Overbuying.** Just because you *can* qualify for more doesn't mean you should. Buy comfortably, not impressively.

2. **Ignoring PCS exit plans.** Before you buy, know your out. Can you rent it easily? Does it cash flow if you leave?

3. **Skipping maintenance and budgeting.** You're a homeowner now, build a reserve fund for repairs and emergencies.

4. **Listening to the wrong people.** Not all lenders or agents understand VA rules. Always work with VA-experienced professionals.

Golden Nugget:
Owning a home is exciting but managing it wisely is what builds wealth.

Real-Life Example: The Assumable Advantage

Let's talk about something most agents barely understand: the **VA loan assumption.**

If you buy a home with a 2.75% VA loan, and years later rates are at 6.5%, that low-rate loan becomes gold. When you sell, another buyer (veteran or civilian) can *assume* your loan, meaning they take over your rate and balance. That makes your home more desirable and valuable.

Even better, it gives you negotiating power in any market. You can use that advantage to build equity faster, attract more buyers, and move into your next home without losing your leverage.

Golden Nugget:
Your interest rate isn't just a number; it's
an asset you can resell.

How to Turn Your BAH Into a Long-Term Game Plan

- **Step 1 – Assess Your Station Timeline.** If you'll be somewhere 2+ years, it's worth running the buy-vs-rent numbers.

- **Step 2 – Get Preapproved with a VA Lender.** Learn your purchasing power and your monthly comfort zone.

- **Step 3 – Find a VA-Savvy Realtor.** Not just any agent, one who understands VA timelines, assumptions, and PCS flexibility.

- **Step 4 – Buy Below Your Max.** Don't stretch your budget to the limit. Leave financial room for real-life expenses; things like maintenance, PCS moves, and future plans.

- **Step 5 – Create a PCS Wealth Plan.** Each move should grow your net worth, not reset it. Think: keep one, buy one.

Golden Nugget Tips

1. **Your BAH is leverage, not luxury**. Don't spend it, build with it.

- **Buy smart, not fast**. Ownership isn't a race; it's a long-term play.

- **Plan every PCS like an investor**. If it can rent, it can pay you.

- **Track your equity**. Watching your wealth grow builds confidence and discipline.

Next Moves

- Look up your current BAH rate and see what mortgage that would support.

- Check your VA loan eligibility and entitlement at VA.gov.

- Schedule a strategy call with a VA-experienced agent to discuss long-term PCS planning.

- Create a 10-year vision: how many homes could you own if you used BAH strategically?

Your BAH isn't just a paycheck, it's a path. Every month, the military pays you to live somewhere. The question is, *will that payment create comfort or wealth?*

- Choose ownership.
- Choose leverage.
- Choose to make your service pay you back for a lifetime.

Chapter 6

Budgeting & Debt Discipline: Gaining Control of Your Financial Mission

Let's be real; most of us didn't join the military because we were financial experts. We joined to serve, to travel, to earn stability, and maybe to grab that college money. But here's the thing: even with steady pay, too many of us still end up asking the same question every pay period: "Where did all my money go?"

If that sounds familiar, this chapter's for you. Budgeting and debt discipline aren't about restriction, they're about freedom. Freedom to make choices. Freedom to invest. Freedom to live without anxiety when your LES drops. Let's break this down, *Ask Antwaun style*.

Budgeting: Your Financial Battle Plan

Every mission starts with a plan. Your money's no different. A budget is simply your **mission order** for each dollar. Without one, you're operating without intel, and that's how you walk into ambushes like overdrafts, late fees, or unnecessary debt.

Here's the simple truth: if you don't tell your money where to go, it'll go everywhere but where you want it.

The 50/30/20 Framework

A solid, simple way to start budgeting is the 50/30/20 rule:

- **50% – Needs:** Rent or mortgage, utilities, groceries, car, insurance.

- **30% – Wants:** Dining out, streaming, travel, hobbies.

- **20% – Savings & Debt Paydown:** Emergency fund, investments, extra debt payments.

This is flexible, but it's a great starting point. You can modify it as your income or goals change.

Golden Nugget:
Budgeting isn't about perfection; it's about awareness. The goal isn't to feel limited; it's to stay intentional.

Step-by-Step Budget Setup

- **Track your expenses for 30 days.** Use your bank app or a budgeting app like Mint, YNAB, or EveryDollar. See where your money *actually* goes, not where you *think* it goes.

- **Calculate your take-home pay.** Include all pay, allowances, and consistent side income.

- **List all monthly obligations.** Mortgage, rent, car, insurance, subscriptions, etc.

- **Prioritize needs, reduce wants.** You don't have to cut everything just trade short-term comfort for long-term gain.

- **Automate your savings.** Set up automatic transfers to your emergency fund or TSP. What you don't see, you won't spend.

- **Review and adjust monthly.** Life changes your budget should, too. Treat it like an after-action review.

Debt Discipline: The Other Side of the Coin

Debt isn't evil, it's a tool. But when mismanaged, it becomes your enemy. Every dollar you owe is a dollar that isn't earning for you. The goal isn't to be *debt-free*; it's to be **debt-wise**. Use debt for leverage, not lifestyle.

Types of Debt: Know Your Enemy

Good Debt – Builds wealth or long-term value.

- Mortgage
- Student loans (for high-ROI education)
- Business loans (with strong potential return)

Bad Debt – Consumes income, adds no lasting value.

- High-interest credit cards

- Payday loans

- Personal loans for "stuff" that depreciates

Golden Nugget:
Debt used strategically is leverage. Debt used emotionally is liability.

How to Attack Debt Strategically

There are two main methods that can help you regain control of your finances:

1. The Debt Snowball Method

- List debts from smallest to largest balance.

- Pay minimums on all but the smallest.

- Throw every extra dollar at that one until it's gone.

- Then roll that payment into the next debt.

This builds momentum and motivation, it's psychological warfare against debt.

2. The Debt Avalanche Method

- List debts by interest rate.

- Pay off the highest rate first, then move down.

This saves the most money in the long run, it's mathematically efficient. Either way, the key is *consistency.*

Golden Nugget:
Pick a method and stick with it. Discipline beats drama.

The Military Advantage: Built-In Financial Stability

Service members have something civilians don't: consistent pay, guaranteed housing allowances, and benefits that create financial predictability. That means you can budget and attack debt with precision.

Here's a simple example:

Sergeant Lee earns $6,000/month (including BAH and BAS). After essentials ($3,000) and wants ($1,500), he has $1,500 left.

He splits that into:

- $750 toward savings and investments

- $750 toward debt payoff

In two years, that's $36,000 redirected toward wealth instead of waste. That's not magic, that's discipline.

Credit: Your Financial Fitness Score

Your credit score is your financial PT test. It determines what you'll pay in interest, whether you qualify for a home, car, or business loan, and sometimes even if you get the apartment you want.

The Five Credit Factors:

- Payment history (35%)
- Credit utilization (30%)
- Credit age (15%)
- Credit mix (10%)
- New inquiries (10%)

Golden Nugget:
Keep utilization below 30%, pay on time, and avoid unnecessary inquiries. Good credit isn't luck, it's habit.

Practical Moves for Debt Discipline

1. **Stop the bleeding.** If you're using credit for everyday needs, pause spending and reassess your budget.

2. **Consolidate wisely.** Look for lower-rate balance transfers or personal loans but only if you stop creating new debt.

3. **Use automatic payments.** Never miss a due date. Consistency builds your credit faster than anything.

4. **Avoid lifestyle inflation.** Every pay raise or promotion doesn't require a spending upgrade.

5. **Protect your security clearance.** Excessive debt or missed payments can risk your clearance and your career.

Golden Nugget:
Money problems don't disappear with rank, they disappear with routine.

Building a Battle-Ready Emergency Fund

An emergency fund is your financial first-aid kit. Aim for 3–6 months of expenses, but start small; even $500 changes your mindset from panic to prepared. This fund keeps you from swiping credit cards when life happens. (Car repairs, PCS costs, or family emergencies.) This is where discipline pays off.

Next Moves

- Track your expenses for the next 30 days to identify waste.

- Create a simple 50/30/20 budget using your actual numbers.

- Choose your debt attack plan. Snowball or Avalanche and start today.

- Automate one habit: savings, TSP, or extra debt payments.

- Celebrate progress, not perfection.

Financial freedom isn't about having more money, it's about having more *control*. When you master your budget and discipline your debt, you gain the ability to move strategically to save, invest, and own on your terms. And that's the real mission: control your money before it controls you.

Chapter 7

Advanced VA Loan Strategies & Assumptions: Playing Chess, Not Checkers

By now, you know the VA loan is one of the most powerful benefits the military offers. But what separates people who *use* it once from those who *leverage* it to build wealth is strategy.

This chapter isn't about getting your first home, it's about turning your VA benefit into a long-term game plan that builds equity, creates options, and multiplies your advantage. It's about playing chess, not checkers.

Understanding the VA Loan Advantage (Recap)

Quick refresher:

- No down payment.

- No PMI.

- Competitive rates.

- Flexible credit standards.

- Reusable benefit.

Those are great. But the hidden power of the VA loan lies in two key features most people never master:

1. Entitlement restoration.

2. Loan assumption.

These two can unlock *multiple homes* and *massive equity growth* throughout your career. Let's break them down.

1. VA Entitlement – Your "Ticket to the Game"

Your VA entitlement is the portion of your loan that the VA guarantees. Think of it like credit from Uncle Sam; it's what allows lenders to offer you those zero-down, low-rate terms.

There are two levels:

- Basic Entitlement: $36,000.

- Bonus Entitlement: Covers higher-priced homes based on county loan limits.

When you use your VA loan, part or all of your entitlement becomes *tied up* in that home. When you sell or refinance out of the VA loan, it can be *restored,* allowing you to use it again.

Golden Nugget:
Your entitlement isn't "used up" forever;
it's reusable once restored.

---

2. Full vs. Partial Entitlement

- **Full Entitlement:** You have no active VA loan, or your prior one was fully repaid and closed.

- **Partial Entitlement:** You still have a VA-backed loan active (for example, you PCS'd and kept the first home as a rental).

With partial entitlement, you can still buy again, just within the remaining guarantee amount. Here's how that looks in real life:

Example:

- You buy a home in Texas for $300,000. The VA guarantees 25% ($75,000).

- You PCS to Virginia and want to buy again for $450,000.

- If your remaining entitlement is $75,000, you may still qualify; you may need a small down payment to cover the difference.

That's how service members end up owning multiple VA-backed homes at once.

Golden Nugget:
Check your remaining entitlement before assuming you "can't buy again." Many veterans qualify for *multiple concurrent* VA loans.

---

3. Entitlement Restoration: How to Reuse the VA Loan

You can restore your entitlement in three ways:

- Sell the property and pay off the VA loan.

- Have a buyer assume your VA loan (more on that next).

- Apply for one-time restoration without selling if the home is paid off but still owned.

This is how you reset your VA benefit to full strength for the next purchase. That's how military homeowners scale one PCS at a time.

Golden Nugget:
Restoration turns your first home into a steppingstone, not a dead end.

---

4. VA Loan Assumptions – The Secret Weapon

Here's where the real power lies: *loan assumptions*. A VA loan assumption means another qualified buyer (veteran or civilian) takes over your existing VA loan with the same balance, same low rate, and same terms.

If you bought when rates were low (say, 2.5–3.5%), that loan becomes an asset. When rates rise to 6–7%, your low-rate mortgage is gold, and buyers will line up for the chance to assume it.

Why It Matters

- You can sell faster and for more money in a high-rate market.

- It makes your listing more attractive than others.

- It helps you preserve your equity even when the market slows.

Golden Nugget:
Your interest rate isn't just a number, it's a negotiation weapon.

---

5. How an Assumption Works

Here's the process in plain English:

1. **Buyer applies** with your loan servicer for approval.

2. **Servicer qualifies** the buyer (credit, income, and debt-to-income check).

3. **If approved,** the buyer takes over your existing loan balance and rate.

4. **They pay you** the difference between your loan balance and the sale price (your equity).

5. **VA releases you** from liability once the assumption is complete.

Example:

- You owe $400,000 on your VA loan at 2.75%.

- You sell your home for $550,000.

- A buyer assumes your $400,000 loan and pays you $150,000 for your equity.

They get your low rate. You get your cash. Everybody wins.

6. Key Considerations for Sellers

If a **civilian** assumes your VA loan, your entitlement stays tied up until they refinance or pay off the loan.

If a **veteran** assumes it and substitutes their own entitlement, yours is restored immediately.

Golden Nugget:
When selling to a civilian, weigh your tradeoff: a fast sale and profit now or entitlement tied up longer.

---

7. The PCS Power Play

Here's how advanced VA users win the game:

- Buy your first home at a low rate.

- PCS, rent it out.

- When ready to sell, market it as VA assumable. That low rate becomes a built-in marketing advantage.

- Use proceeds and/or restored entitlement to buy the next property with no down payment.

That's how you leapfrog from one station to the next, building equity, rental income, and a portfolio funded entirely by service benefits.

Golden Nugget:
Every PCS can either restart your finances or accelerate your wealth. The choice is strategy.

---

8. Protecting Your VA Advantage

1. Always confirm release of liability when someone assumes your loan.

2. Track your entitlement through VA.gov after every sale or assumption.

3. Work with VA-experienced lenders and agents. Not every professional understands entitlement math or assumption processing.

4. Stay informed. VA rules evolve. Knowing them first keeps you ahead.

9. Example: The Compound PCS Strategy

Let's say you start your career in Georgia and buy your first home with a VA loan at 3%. Five years later, you PCS to Hawaii. You rent out the Georgia home, use partial entitlement for a new purchase, and buy again with no down payment.

When you PCS again to California, you sell the Georgia home. The buyer assumes your low-rate loan, restoring your entitlement. You now buy a third home in California using your full entitlement again.

Each move created equity, cash flow, and appreciation. By the time you retire, you've built a small real estate portfolio funded by your BAH and PCS orders. That's not luck. That's **Ask Antwaun level strategy.**

Golden Nugget Tips

1. **Your rate is leverage.** A 3% mortgage in a 7% market adds value to your home.

2. **You can have more than one VA loan.** Understand partial entitlement before assuming you can't.

3. **Sell smart.** Always request release of liability after an assumption.

4. **Plan long-term.** Think beyond the next move. Every home should serve your future financial mission.

Next Moves

- Check your VA Certificate of Eligibility (COE) to confirm entitlement.

- Review your loan's assumability with your servicer. Get written details.

- If you're planning to PCS, calculate potential rent and resale scenarios early.

- Talk to a VA-savvy agent to build an exit strategy that fits your timeline.

- Keep a running spreadsheet of your homes, balances, and entitlement usage. Treat it like your own "real estate battle plan."

The VA loan isn't a one-time key; it's a master key. It opens doors across your career, one station at a time. The difference between average and advanced isn't opportunity. Its strategy. Don't just use your benefits. *Leverage them.*

Chapter 8

Passive Income & Multiple Streams: Earning While You Serve

Let's be honest, in the military, "passive" isn't a word we hear often. Our lives are about structure, schedules, and hustle. But when it comes to money? Passive is exactly what you want. Because real financial freedom happens when your money earns money even while you sleep, deploy, or PCS. That's what passive income is all about. It's not how much you make that matters; it's how much keeps working when you don't.

Why You Need Multiple Streams of Income

The average millionaire has seven streams of income. Most service members have one, their paycheck. That's a dangerous place to stay. All it takes is one injury, one contract change, or one transition to shake your foundation.

Having multiple income streams doesn't mean that you're chasing side hustles; it means you're building systems. Systems that keep paying you whether you're on orders, in training, or retired.

1. Real Estate: The Foundation of Passive Income

You already know where I'm going with this. Real estate is the most proven, repeatable way to build passive income, and your VA loan gives you a head start.

Here's how to do it strategically:

- **A. Live-In First, Rent Later (The PCS Strategy)**. Buy your home using your VA loan, live in it for a year (to meet occupancy requirements), and when you PCS, rent it out.

- That property now pays you every month while someone else pays down your mortgage.

Golden Nugget:
If your BAH covered your mortgage while
you lived there, your tenant can cover it
when you leave, turning your PCS into a
passive income stream.

B. Short-Term Rentals (When Allowed)

If your location or HOA allows, turning your
property into a furnished short-term rental can
multiply returns.

Think TDY travelers, vacationers, or military
families waiting for housing. Just make sure you
understand local rules and manage it responsi-
bly.

C. Multi-Unit Properties

The VA loan allows up to four units as long as
you live in one. You can rent the other units, often
covering your entire mortgage with rental income.
That's called house hacking, and it's one of the
fastest ways to build equity and cash flow.

Golden Nugget:
You don't have to wait until retirement to be a landlord; your service already qualifies you to start.

---

2. Digital & Knowledge-Based Income

You don't need to own real estate to earn passively. You can also build digital assets that pay long after the work is done.

- **Online Courses or E-Books:** Teach what you know, such as leadership, fitness, cybersecurity, and military transition, and sell it on platforms like Udemy or Gumroad.

- **Affiliate Marketing:** Earn commissions by recommending tools, books, or services you already use.

- **Content Creation:** YouTube, podcasts, or blogs can build steady ad revenue over time.

Golden Nugget:
The internet never PCS's. It can help you build something once and it can pay you from anywhere.

---

3. Dividend & Interest Income

If you've been investing through your TSP, Roth IRA, or brokerage, you're already earning passive income; you just might not recognize it.

- **Dividends:** Paid by companies or ETFs just for owning their stock.

- **Interest:** Earned from bonds, high-yield savings, or peer-to-peer lending.

Reinvest those earnings, and you've got compound growth working for you in the background. That's quiet wealth.

4. Business Ownership (The Semi-Passive Way)

Entrepreneurship doesn't always mean quitting your job. You can own or invest in a business that operates without your full-time involvement.

Some examples:

- Vending or laundry machines on base or in local housing.

- Car washes, mobile detailing, or storage facilities.

- Partnering with a trusted operator who runs the day-to-day.

Golden Nugget:
Passive income doesn't mean "no work." It means build once, benefit repeatedly.

---

5. Licensing, Royalties, and Side Projects

Got a skill or creative streak? Protect it and get paid for it.

- License your photography or music.

- Develop an app or tool for your field.

- Write a training guide or manual that can be resold or licensed to organizations.

The military builds discipline, consistency, and problem-solving. those are the same skills that create intellectual property.

6. The Hybrid Approach: Active Duty, Passive Hustle

You don't have to wait until your ETS to start. Use your stability and benefits to build now:

- Steady pay = predictable cash flow for investments.

- BAH = free housing leverage.

- TSP = automatic long-term wealth.

- SkillBridge or transition programs = free business or education prep.

Golden Nugget:
Your active-duty years are your wealth-building runway. Use it.

---

7. Managing Multiple Streams

With multiple streams, structure matters. Here's how to stay organized:

1. **Separate accounts** for business, rental, and personal income.

2. **Track cash flow** with apps like QuickBooks, Mint, or Google Sheets.

3. **Save for taxes.** If you earn income outside the military, set aside 20–25%.

4. **Automate reinvestment.** Let your profits feed your next opportunity.

Golden Nugget:
Treat your income streams like troops.
Train them, track them, and make them
work together toward the mission.

---

8. Avoiding the "Shiny Object" Trap

When you start earning extra, it's easy to want to do *everything*: crypto, dropshipping, real estate, stocks, side hustles all at once. Don't.

Focus on building one solid stream before starting the next. Diversification is smart, *distraction is deadly.*

Golden Nugget:
Multiple streams don't mean multiple
distractions. Build one, master it, then
multiply.

Next Moves

1. Identify one income stream you can start this year.

2. Create a one-page "wealth plan." List every stream you have or want.

3. Automate your savings or investment contributions.

4. Join a community (online or local) of other investors or entrepreneurs for accountability.

5. Reinvest at least 10% of every new income stream back into another.

Passive income isn't about getting rich quick, it's about getting *free slowly*. The same discipline you've used in uniform is the same discipline that will build your financial freedom.

You already know how to serve with purpose; now it's time to let your money do the same.

Chapter 9

Retirement & Transition Planning: Building Freedom Beyond the Uniform

Leaving the military hits everyone differently. For some, it's excitement about new beginnings and new opportunities. For others, it's anxiety: the paycheck, the structure, and the purpose you've known for years suddenly changes.

I've been there. When I transitioned out after 13 years, I thought I was prepared. I had a good civilian job lined up, solid pay, and plenty of experience. But what I didn't have was a plan for my freedom, not just a plan for employment.

That's what this chapter is about: turning your career, benefits, and discipline into long-term wealth and peace of mind. Because retiring or separating from service isn't the end of your financial mission; it's just the next phase.

Step 1: Redefine What "Retirement" Means

Most people think retirement means stopping work. For us, it's different. It means having the option to stop working, not the obligation to.

Financial freedom is about choice. Whether you retire after 20 years or separate after 8, your goal should be the same:

Have more income coming in than expenses going out without needing a paycheck. That's real freedom. That's when your service starts paying you back.

Step 2: Know Your Military Retirement System

Depending on when you joined, you fall under one of two main systems:

1. Legacy (High-3) Retirement System

- You earn 2.5% of your highest 36 months of base pay per year of service.

- 20 years = 50% of your base pay for life.

2. Blended Retirement System (BRS)

- You earn 2% of your base pay per year of service. 20 years = 40% of base pay for life.

- **PLUS** government TSP match (up to 5%).

If you're under BRS, contributing at least 5% to your TSP is non-negotiable. That's free money and your future retirement engine.

Golden Nugget:
Your pension is the floor, not the ceiling.
Build streams of income *above* it.

Step 3: Estimate Your Post-Service Expenses
When you leave the military, some benefits stop or shrink:

- No more BAH or BAS.

- You may pay more for healthcare.

- You'll have to cover relocation, taxes, and retirement contributions on your own.

That's why your budget should be based on **civilian costs**, not your LES comfort zone.

Start by mapping out your baseline:

- Housing

- Healthcare (Tricare or civilian coverage)

- Groceries, utilities, transportation
- Taxes and insurance
- Savings and investments

Golden Nugget:

Don't plan to survive after service; plan to thrive. Budget for comfort, not survival.

Step 4: Leverage What You've Already Built

If you've followed the earlier chapters, by now you've got:

- A **TSP** growing quietly in the background.
- One or more **properties** generating cash flow or equity.
- A **budget** that keeps you disciplined.
- A few **income streams** that don't rely on your uniform.

Your job now is to connect the dots and turn assets into lifestyle freedom.

Your Income Pyramid After Service

1. **Base Level:** Pension + TSP withdrawals

2. **Middle Level:** Rental income, dividends, side business profits

3. **Top Level:** Passive income from investments, royalties, or digital assets

When you can live off the middle and top layers, the bottom layer becomes your safety net, not your lifeline.

Golden Nugget:
Freedom isn't built in one move; it's stacked, layer by layer.

Step 5: Use Transition Tools to Your Advantage

The military gives you more help than most realize, but you've got to take advantage of it.

- TAP (Transition Assistance Program): Attend early. Take it seriously.

- SkillBridge: Use your final 180 days to intern or train with civilian companies.

- Education Benefits: The GI Bill and Tuition Assistance can fund new skills or certifications.

- VA Resources: Use your VA Home Loan, healthcare, and disability benefits wisely.

Golden Nugget:
Your benefits are *assets*. Stop leaving them on the table.

Step 6: Protect Your Wealth

You spent years building it; now guard it like you guarded your team.

- **Insurance:** Life, health, and property protection.

- **Estate Planning:** Will, trust, and power of attorney.

- **Taxes:** Understand how your new income streams are taxed and plan ahead.

- **Emergency Fund:** Keep 3-6 months of expenses liquid. Transition costs can sneak up on you.

Golden Nugget:
The same way you maintain readiness in uniform, maintain financial readiness in retirement.

Step 7: Plan Your Purpose

Transitioning isn't just financial, it's emotional. For years, your identity has been tied to service. Now it's time to define what's next.

Ask yourself:

- What do I want to do with my time and skills?

- Who do I want to impact?

- What kind of legacy do I want to leave?

Whether that means starting a business, mentoring others, or just living on your terms plan for purpose, not just paychecks.

Golden Nugget:
Your next mission doesn't have to come with rank, just purpose.

Step 8: Design Your Exit Strategy

Here's your transition checklist:

1. 2 Years Before Transition:

- Maximize TSP contributions.

- Pay off or consolidate high-interest debt.

- Research SkillBridge, certifications, or business ideas.

2. 1 Year Before:

  - Meet with a financial planner (preferably one who understands military benefits).
  - Get updated copies of all your service records and VA documents.
  - Begin applying for VA disability if applicable.

3. 6 Months Before:

  - Lock in post-service housing plans.
  - Finalize your healthcare and insurance coverage.
  - Set up your civilian or business accounts for income continuity.

At Transition: Execute your financial plan. Budget, track, and reassess every 90 days.

Golden Nugget:
Don't wait until separation to start planning. Your financial transition begins *years* before your ETS date.

Next Moves

- Log in to your TSP and review your projected balance at different retirement ages.

- Start mapping your post-service monthly expenses.

- Create your own "Freedom Budget" based on lifestyle goals, not just survival needs.

- Schedule a free consultation with a VA-accredited financial planner or transition specialist.

- Decide what your next mission will be and design your money to fund it.

Your military career gave you discipline, structure, and leadership, all the traits needed to succeed in civilian life. Now it's time to apply them to your financial freedom.

Your benefits, investments, and income streams aren't just for survival; they're the foundation of your next chapter. Retirement isn't the finish line. It's the launchpad. And the best part? You've already earned the tools to build the life you want.

Chapter 10

Legacy & Wealth Transfer: Building What Outlives You

By this point, you've learned how to make your money, save it, invest it, and multiply it. But wealth alone isn't the end goal; it's what you do with it that counts. When you hang up the uniform, your mission doesn't end. It just shifts.

Now your mission is to protect what you've built and pass it forward to your family, your community, and the next generation of service members following behind you.

That's legacy.

The Real Meaning of Legacy

Legacy isn't just about money. It's about impact. It's the lessons, values, and example you leave behind. The financial part is just the tool, the vehicle that carries your influence beyond your lifetime.

A paycheck ends when you stop working. A legacy keeps paying your family in money, knowledge, and opportunity. When your kids understand ownership, when your spouse feels secure, and when your community sees what's possible, that's wealth in motion.

1. From Wealth Building to Wealth Keeping

You've spent years learning how to earn and invest. Now it's time to protect it. There's a simple rule. It's not what you make; it's what you keep, protect, and pass on that builds legacy. Here's how to start.

A. Create a Will

A will is your final set of orders. It ensures your assets, property, and wishes are handled exactly how you want. Without one, your family may face legal challenges and delays during an already emotional time. You can create one through:

- Base legal office (for free while serving)
- Online legal services
- A private estate attorney for complex assets

B. Set Up a Trust (If Applicable)

A trust keeps your estate private, avoids probate (the long court process), and can distribute your wealth over time instead of all at once. It's especially useful if you own multiple properties or plan to leave inheritances for children.

Golden Nugget:

A will says *who* gets what. A trust controls *how* and *when* they get it.

---

2. Protecting Your Family Financially

A legacy starts with protection, making sure your family is covered no matter what.

Life Insurance

You likely have SGLI (Servicemembers' Group Life Insurance) or VGLI (Veterans' Group Life Insurance). That's a great foundation, but you can also add private coverage that builds cash value or lasts for life, not just your service years.

- Term insurance covers you for a set period (cheaper, straightforward).

- Whole life or indexed universal life policies build cash value you can access later.

Golden Nugget:
Life insurance isn't just protection, it's a tool for legacy planning and tax-free wealth transfer.

Disability & Long-Term Care

These often get overlooked, but one injury or illness can drain your savings faster than you'd expect. Military and VA benefits are strong, but supplemental coverage can protect your family's long-term stability.

3. Teaching Financial Literacy at Home

The most valuable inheritance you can give your kids isn't cash, it's *competence*. They need to understand money the way you do now. Start with small lessons:

- Let them see you budget and explain why.

- Teach them about saving vs. spending.

- Open a custodial savings or investment account in their name.

If your kids grow up understanding leverage, ownership, and discipline, they'll multiply your legacy far beyond what you could do alone.

Golden Nugget:
Generational wealth isn't about
inheritance, it's about *education* passed
down with it.

---

4. Creating Generational Leverage

Here's how the wealthy think differently. They
don't aim to leave money. They aim to leave momentum. That means building systems that keep
producing after you're gone.

Example Plan:

- Properties that cash flow to your family.

- A trust that funds your kids' education or
  business start-up.

- Investments that generate dividends to
  cover family expenses.

- Insurance policies that replace your lifetime earnings.

You're building not just assets. You're building
infrastructure.

Golden Nugget:
You can't pass down your BAH or LES, but
you can pass down what you built with
them.

---

5. Give While You're Alive

Legacy isn't just what happens when you're gone, it's what you do *while you're here.* Use your success to lift others.

Ways to give back:

- Mentor young service members on financial literacy.
- Donate to veteran housing or education programs.
- Help a family member make their first down payment.
- Support local organizations that serve the military community.

When you share what you've learned, you multiply your impact.

Golden Nugget:
A legacy isn't what you leave *behind,* it's what you set in *motion.*

---

6. Preparing Your Family for the Transfer

We've seen it happen too many times: someone passes away, and their family has no idea what to do next. Don't let that happen to yours.

Create a "Legacy Binder," a simple packet that includes:

- Your will or trust
- Life insurance policy info
- Property deeds
- VA and military benefits details
- Account passwords and contact info for key professionals.

Keep it in a safe place and update it yearly. Then, and this is key, talk about it with your immediate family. Don't keep your family in the dark about your plan. Transparency prevents confusion and conflict later.

Golden Nugget:
The best legacy plan isn't a surprise; it's a conversation.

---

7. Legacy Beyond Family: Community Impact

Your story, your service, and your success carry weight. You've walked a path few understand, and your example can change lives. Think about how to pour back into your community:

- Teach financial readiness at your base or veterans' center.

- Partner with organizations that support transitioning service members.

- Sponsor youth programs that promote discipline and leadership.

The ripple effect of your story can reach further than your bank account ever could.

Golden Nugget:
Your money builds comfort. Your example builds courage.

Next Moves

1. Schedule an appointment with your base legal office or estate attorney.

2. Create a written will and review life insurance coverage.

3. Start teaching your kids or spouse one financial concept a month.

4. Build your "Legacy Binder" keep it updated and secure.

5. Identify one way you can give back or mentor others this year.

Closing Message

You started this journey to learn how to use your benefits and build wealth. Now you've learned that real wealth isn't just what's in your account; it's what you create for others.

The same discipline that built your career can build generational change. You've served your country; now it's time to serve your future.

Your story matters. Your legacy matters. And it all starts with one decision: to take what you've earned and make it work for you, for your family, and for generations to come.

Chapter 11

Wealth Building Case Studies: Success Stories from the Ranks

The military is full of people grinding hard every day, some just trying to make ends meet, others quietly building empires. Same paycheck. Same BAH. Same opportunities. The difference? Strategy.

In this chapter, I want to show you how service members from E-4s to officers used the same tools you have to build *real* wealth.

These are not celebrities or overnight millionaires. They are soldiers, airmen, sailors, and Marines who decided to play the money game differently.

Case Study 1: The PCS Investor

- **Rank:** Staff Sergeant (E-6)

- **Branch:** U.S. Army
- **Stationed:** Fort Hood → Fort Carson → Schofield Barracks

When SSG Taylor bought his first home in Texas, it was just a place to live: a $235,000 starter home with a VA loan at 2.75%.

Two years later, PCS orders hit. Instead of selling, he rented it out for $1,900/month while his mortgage was $1,450.

At his next duty station, he used *partial entitlement* to buy another home again, with zero down. He repeated the process every PCS.

Now, eight years later, Taylor owns three homes across three states, each with equity growth and positive cash flow. When he retires, his properties will produce over $3,000 a month in passive income, his own personal pension.

Golden Nugget:
Turn every PCS into an opportunity. The military moves you let those moves build your portfolio.

Case Study 2: The "BAH Means Buy A House" Couple

- **Rank:** Dual E-5s (Married Couple)
- **Branch:** U.S. Navy

When the Garcias first heard about using their BAH to build wealth, they thought homeownership was out of reach. They lived on base and spent their BAH on travel and lifestyle.

After a base housing waitlist delay, they decided to buy. Using both incomes, they purchased a $420,000 home near San Diego, using their combined BAH to cover the mortgage, every cent of it.

Fast forward five years: they've built over $180,000 in equity. When rates jumped, their 2.9% mortgage became their biggest asset.

They're now PCSing to Virginia and plan to rent that home for $3,200/month, covering their mortgage and generating profit.

Golden Nugget:

BAH isn't just housing allowance, it's leverage. You can spend it, or you can own with it.

Case Study 3: The Early Investor Who Used the TSP Like a Pro

- **Rank:** Specialist (E-4)
- **Branch:** U.S. Army Reserve

At 22, SPC Johnson decided to contribute 10% of her pay to the TSP. Her peers laughed. "That's only for retirement."

Ten years later, she's sitting on $115,000 in her account before age 33. That money has grown through compound interest, government matching, and consistent deposits.

She plans to roll that balance into a Roth IRA and start investing in dividend-paying stocks after ETS. Her TSP became her foundation for long-term freedom.

Golden Nugget:
Consistency beats intensity. Start small, stay steady, and time will do the heavy lifting.

Case Study 4: The VA Loan Assumption Win

- **Rank:** Warrant Officer (CW2)
- **Branch:** U.S. Army Aviation

When CW2 Evans bought his home in 2020 at 2.5%, he had no idea that loan would become one of his most valuable assets.

In 2024, he got orders to PCS and listed his property as VA assumable. Within two weeks, he had multiple offers, not because of the house, but because of the rate.

He sold his home for $40,000 above asking price to a civilian buyer who assumed his VA loan. CW2 Evans walked away with $150,000 in equity, restored his entitlement, and used it to buy a new home at his next duty station again with no down payment.

Golden Nugget:
Your low-rate mortgage is more than a loan, it's a marketing advantage. In a high-rate market, it's gold.

Case Study 5: The Debt-Free Sergeant
- **Rank:** Sergeant (E-5)
- **Branch:** U.S. Marine Corps

Sgt. Brooks was tired of living paycheck to paycheck. He started tracking every dollar using the 50/30/20 rule and attacked his $18,000 credit card balance using the Debt Snowball Method.

He paid off his smallest debt first, then rolled that payment into the next one. It took 18 months, but when he finished, he freed up $700 a month.

That $700 now goes into his high-yield savings and TSP. Two years later, he has $20,000 saved and zero consumer debt.

Golden Nugget:
Discipline is the bridge between broke and built. Your budget is your battle plan.

Case Study 6: The Civilian Transition Strategist

- **Rank:** Captain (O-3)

- **Branch:** U.S. Air Force

Capt. Nguyen knew her ETS date two years out and started planning early. She maxed out her TSP, took SkillBridge with a defense contractor, and used her VA home loan to buy a duplex near her new job.

She lives in one unit, rents out the other, and now her tenant covers **70% of her mortgage**. Her military benefits transitioned seamlessly into civilian financial independence.

Golden Nugget:
Transition isn't an ending, it's a transfer of skills and strategy. Plan early, move smart.

Case Study 7: The Legacy Builder

- **Rank:** Retired Senior Chief (E-8)
- **Branch:** U.S. Navy

After 24 years of service, Senior Chief Morales retired with a pension and three properties purchased during his career.

But his real success? He taught his kids everything he learned. His oldest son bought his first duplex at 25 using a VA loan. His daughter opened a Roth IRA at 18. He didn't just leave money, he left *knowledge*.

Golden Nugget:
Generational wealth isn't measured in dollars, it's measured in understanding.
Teach as you earn.

Case Study 8: The "Ask Antwaun" Blueprint

- **Rank:** Veteran (Former CW2)

- **Branch:** U.S. Army

I'll close with my own journey because I've lived both sides of this. I was that soldier who used to spend every cent. I saw others building wealth and wondered how.

It wasn't until I learned that wealth isn't built from how much you make but how you manage what you have that things changed.

Once I got intentional about budgeting, investing, and using my VA benefits, everything shifted. Now, I teach others to do the same. And that's why this book exists. To show that it's not about luck, it's about *leverage*.

Golden Nugget:
The difference between struggling and succeeding isn't opportunity, it's understanding.

Next Moves

- Identify one story in this chapter that mirrors your situation.

- Write down the *one action* they took that you can apply this month.

- Track your progress for 90 days one disciplined step at a time.

- Remember: you don't have to be rich to start. You have to start to get rich.

These stories prove that wealth building isn't theory, it's a choice. Every rank, every branch, every paycheck holds potential when paired with discipline and strategy. You don't need a financial advisor to start, you just need awareness and a plan. Your benefits are the blueprint. Your habits are the engine.

The same drive that got you through basic, deployments, and promotion boards is the same drive that can create financial freedom.

Chapter 12

Creating Your Action Plan: Steps to Financial Independence

You've come a long way. You've learned how to make your money, save it, invest it, and multiply it. Now, it's time to *execute*.

This chapter is your blueprint, not to read, but to *use*. Grab a pen. Write in this book. Make it yours. Because financial independence doesn't happen by accident, it happens by design.

Mission Objective: Financial Freedom

Definition:

Financial independence = income from assets and passive sources covers your living expenses without needing a paycheck. That's when you own your time. That's when you control your choices. That's when your service starts paying *you back*.

Step 1: Know Your Financial Starting Point

You can't fix or grow what you don't measure. This is your baseline, your financial "situation report." Write it out below. Be honest.

Monthly Income:

- Base Pay: _____
- Allowances (BAH/BAS): _____
- Other Income: _____
- **Total Monthly Income:** _____

Monthly Expenses:

- Housing: _____
- Car/Transportation: _____
- Food/Groceries: _____
- Utilities/Subscriptions: _____
- Debt Payments: _____
- Other: _____
- Total Monthly Expenses: _____

- Current Debt Total: _____
- Current Savings/Investments: _____

Golden Nugget:
You can't move forward if you don't know your coordinates. Start with the truth, no judgment, just data.

Step 2: Build Your Financial Battle Plan

Every mission needs structure. This plan is yours, your personal operation order for money.

List what you'll focus on first:

- ☐ Budgeting
- ☐ Saving
- ☐ Investing
- ☐ Using VA/TSP benefits
- ☐ Protecting what you build

My Primary Focus for the Next 90 Days:

_____

_____

_____
_____
_____
_____
_____
_____
_____
_____
_____
_____
_____
_____
_____
_____
_____

Golden Nugget:
You don't have to do everything at once just start with one mission and execute it well.

Step 3: Set Clear Financial Goals

Be specific. Numbers don't lie, and they keep you accountable.

Short-Term Goals (6–12 months):

_____

_____

_____

_____

_____

_____

_____

_____

_____

_____

Mid-Term Goals (1–5 years):

_____

_____

_____

_____

_____

_____

_____

_____

_____

_____

Long-Term Goals (10+ years):

_____

_____

_____

_____

_____

_____

_____

_____

_____

Golden Nugget:
Don't chase money. Chase milestones.

Step 4: Automate Your Progress

Set up systems that work without thinking.

I will automate:

☐ Savings transfer of $_____ every payday

☐ TSP contributions of _____ %

☐ Debt payments for these accounts: _____

☐ Bill payments for: _____

Start Date: _____

Review Date: _____

Golden Nugget:
Systems beat willpower every time.

Step 5: Eliminate Toxic Debt

Write out every debt you have. Then choose your attack method:

☐ **Snowball** (smallest balance first)

☐ **Avalanche** (highest interest first)

Debt	Balance	Interest Rate	Plan of Attack	Monthly Payment
_____	_____	_____	_____	_____
_____	_____	_____	_____	_____
_____	_____	_____	_____	_____
_____	_____	_____	_____	_____
_____	_____	_____	_____	_____
_____	_____	_____	_____	_____

Debt	Balance	Interest Rate	Plan of Attack	Monthly Payment
_____	_____	_____	_____	_____
_____	_____	_____	_____	_____
_____	_____	_____	_____	_____
_____	_____	_____	_____	_____
_____	_____	_____	_____	_____
_____	_____	_____	_____	_____

Target	Payoff	Date:
_____	_____	_____
_____	_____	_____
_____	_____	_____
_____	_____	_____
_____	_____	_____
_____	_____	_____
_____	_____	_____

Golden Nugget:

Debt is a tool, not a lifestyle. Control it before it controls you.

Step 6: Build Your Emergency Fund

Your emergency fund is your safety net, not your vacation fund.

Goal:

☐ Starter Fund: $1,000

☐ 3–6 months of living expenses: $_____

Where I'll keep it (bank name or account type):

_____

_____

Automatic Monthly Contribution: $_____

Golden Nugget:
If you don't have an emergency fund, every small problem becomes a financial crisis.

Step 7: Use Your VA Loan Strategically

You already earned one of the best home-buying tools in America. Use it wisely.

Current Home: _____

Rate: % | *Loan Balance:* $_____

Plan:

☐ Keep and Rent Out

☐ Sell and Restore Entitlement

☐ Explore Assumption

Next Purchase Goal: _____

Estimated Timeline: _____

Golden Nugget:
Your VA loan isn't a one-time benefit, it's a
lifetime weapon for building equity.

Step 8: Grow Multiple Streams of Income

List your current income sources and the next
one you'll build.

Stream	Type	Monthly Income	Next Action
_____	_____	_____	_____
_____	_____	_____	_____
_____	_____	_____	_____
_____	_____	_____	_____
_____	_____	_____	_____
_____	_____	_____	_____

Next Income Stream I'll Build:

_____

_____

_____

_____

_____

_____

Start Date: _____

Golden Nugget:
Multiple paychecks = multiple levels of
protection.

Step 9: Review & Adjust Quarterly

Set a recurring date to check your progress. Think of it like your Financial After-Action Review (AAR).

Next	Review	Date:
_____	_____	_____
_____	_____	_____
_____	_____	_____
_____	_____	_____
_____	_____	_____

Wins Since Last Review:

_____

_____

_____

_____

_____

_____

_____

_____

_____

_____

_____

Adjustments Needed:

_____

_____

_____

_____

_____

_____

_____

_____

_____

_____

_____

_____

_____

Golden Nugget:
If you're not reviewing your plan, you're repeating your mistakes.

Step 10: Build for Legacy

Plan beyond yourself. This is how you make wealth *last*.

☐ Update my will or trust

☐ Review life insurance

☐ Create/Update my Legacy Binder

☐ Teach my family one money concept this month

Who I'll Teach or Mentor:

_____

_____

_____

_____

_____

_____

_____

_____

_____

Legacy Goal:

_____

_____

_____

_____

_____

_____

_____

_____

_____

Golden Nugget:
Legacy isn't what you leave behind, it's
what you set in motion.
_____

Your 90-Day Action Plan Summary
My Top 3 Financial Missions:

1. _____

_____

_____

2. _____

_____

_____

3. _____

_____

_____

Antwaun Hill

Accountability Partner (Optional): _____

Signature   Date:

_____   _____

    This is your contract with yourself. You've done the reading; now you've got the roadmap. Every paycheck is a choice: spend it, save it, or make it work for you. Make this the moment where knowledge becomes action. And when you need guidance, you already know who to ask.

Epilogue

Your Next Mission

If you made it to this point, I want you to take a second and be proud of yourself. Seriously, most people never take the time to understand their money, their benefits, or their potential. But you did. You showed up. You took the time to learn.

That means you're different not because of what's in your bank account, but because of what's in your mindset.

When I look back at my own journey from an 18-year-old kid stepping off a bus at Fort Jackson to a Warrant Officer trying to figure out how the hell to build a future, I realize I was chasing all the wrong things.

I thought stability came from rank. I thought wealth came from working harder. I thought success came with time served. But what I learned is this: wealth doesn't come from service, it comes from strategy. And every one of us has access to it.

Your benefits, your pay, and your BAH are not just perks. They're weapons. And this book was never about money; it's about leverage. The kind of leverage that gives your family freedom, your future options, and your life purpose beyond the uniform. So whether you're still in the fight, fresh out, or already retired, your mission isn't over. It's evolving. You've defended your country. Now it's time to defend your future.

Your Call to Action...

When you close this book, don't just go back to business as usual. Do something.

- ☑ Open that TSP account.
- ☑ Schedule that meeting with your base legal office.
- ☑ Start the process for your VA loan.
- ☑ Write down your 90-day plan in the back of this book.
- ☑ Talk to your family about your financial goals.

One action at a time. That's how you build wealth. That's how you build legacy.

Final Words

You've got everything you need inside you already, the discipline, the grit, the commitment, and the heart. The same qualities that made you successful in uniform will make you unstoppable in life.

You've served your country. Now serve your future, serve your family, and serve your purpose. And when you need clarity, when you hit a wall, when you start to doubt if it's possible, you already know where to turn.

Because remember, knowledge is leverage.

Need answers?
Just Ask Antwaun

Ready to put your plan in motion? Scan below to set up your free strategy session with Antwaun Hill.

Resources and Tools for Financial Success

You've built the mindset. You've written your action plan. Now it's time to give you the tools to make it happen. Because knowing what to do is half the battle. Having the right tools to execute is how you win the war.

This chapter is your toolkit. Bookmark it. Print it. Use it. Share it. And most importantly, come back to it whenever you need to reset or refocus.

1. Budgeting & Expense Tracking Tools

Apps & Websites

- **Mint.com** – Free app that syncs with your bank accounts, tracks spending, and categorizes expenses automatically.

- **You Need a Budget (YNAB)** – Helps you give every dollar a job; perfect for intentional spending.

- **EveryDollar** – Created by Dave Ramsey's team; simple zero-based budgeting tool.

- **Google Sheets / Excel Templates** – Easy to customize for monthly cash flow and military LES tracking.

Golden Nugget:
Budgeting is your situational awareness. Know where every dollar is positioned before the mission starts.

---

2. Saving & Emergency Fund Tools

High-Yield Online Banks

- **Ally Bank** – Easy transfers, no monthly fees, competitive savings rate.

- **Discover Bank** – High APY and excellent mobile app.

- **Navy Federal Credit Union** – Military-friendly, strong customer support.

- **USAA Savings** – Seamless with military pay; integrates with checking and insurance.

Goal Tracker

- Emergency Fund Target: $_____

- Current Savings: _____
- Monthly Auto-Transfer: $_____
- Target Completion Date: _____

Golden Nugget:

Don't overthink saving. Automate it once and forget it. Let time do the work.

---

3. Investing & Retirement Planning Resources

Thrift Savings Plan (TSP)

- Website: tsp.gov
- Use the **TSP Calculator** to project growth over time.
- Key Tip: Contribute at least 5% to get the full government match under BRS.

Investment Tools

- **Personal Capital** – Free portfolio tracker and retirement planner.
- **Morningstar.com** – Research mutual funds and ETFs.
- **Fidelity & Vanguard** – Great for Roth IRAs, index funds, and low-cost investing.

Learn As You Earn

- "The Simple Path to Wealth" by JL Collins
- "Rich Dad Poor Dad" by Robert Kiyosaki
- "Your Money or Your Life" by Joe Dominguez

Golden Nugget:
Investing isn't timing the market, it's time *in* the market that wins.

---

4. Real Estate & VA Loan Tools

VA Loan Calculators

- Guaranty Percentage Calculator
  https://lgy.va.gov/lgyhub/guaranty-calcu-lator
- Veterans United Mortgage Estimator
  https://www.veteransunited.com/educa-tion/tools/mortgage-calculator/
- NerdWallet Mortgage Calculator
  https://www.nerdwallet.com/mort-gages/mortgage-calculator

Must-Know Contacts

- **Base Legal Office:** For free will & trust setup.

- **Housing Office:** For BAH rate verification and PCS housing options.

- **Loan Officer / Realtor:** Find VA-experienced professionals before you shop.

House Hack Worksheet

Property	Loan Type	Rate	Monthly Payment	Rent Income	Net Cash Flow
___	___	___	___	___	___
___	___	___	___	___	___
___	___	___	___	___	___
___	___	___	___	___	___
___	___	___	___	___	___
___	___	___	___	___	___

Golden Nugget:
You don't have to buy your dream home first buy the home that funds your dreams later.

5. Credit & Debt Management Tools

Free Credit Resources

- **AnnualCreditReport.com** – Get your free credit report from all three bureaus once per year.

- **Credit Karma / Experian / NerdWallet** – Track your score and utilization monthly.

Debt Reduction Tools

- **Undebt.it** – Build a custom snowball or avalanche debt plan.

- **Debt Payoff Planner App** – Track balances, payments, and milestones visually.

Quick Debt Snapshot

Account	Balance	Interest	Minimum Payment
_____	_____	_____	_____
_____	_____	_____	_____
_____	_____	_____	_____
_____	_____	_____	_____
_____	_____	_____	_____
_____	_____	_____	_____

Golden Nugget:
Debt payoff isn't a sprint, it's a strategic withdrawal from financial enemy territory.

---

6. Insurance & Protection Resources

Military & Veteran Options

- **SGLI / VGLI:** Servicemembers' and Veterans' Group Life Insurance

- **USAA / Navy Federal:** Offer term and whole life options

- **AUSA / AMBA:** Group plans for retired or transitioning service members

Protection Checklist

☐ Life insurance policy reviewed within 12 months

☐ Disability coverage in place

☐ Updated will/trust filed

☐ Beneficiaries current on all accounts

Golden Nugget:

You built the wealth, now guard it like your gear.

---

7. Education & Career Transition Resources

Education Benefits

- **GI Bill Comparison Tool:**

  VA.gov/gi-bill-comparison-tool

- **MyCAA:** For military spouses seeking career training grants.

- **SkillBridge:** DoD program allowing active-duty members to intern during final 180 days.

Transition Resources

- **TAP (Transition Assistance Program)** – Mandatory but underutilized. Attend early.

- **Hire Heroes USA / Onward to Opportunity** – Free job placement and career coaching.

- **Bunker Labs / Vetpreneur Tribe** – Veteran entrepreneur communities and funding support.

Golden Nugget:
Your transition isn't the end of your service, it's the beginning of your success.

---

8. Legacy & Estate Planning Resources

Legal & Planning Tools
- **Base Legal Office:** Free for active-duty and retirees.
- **Rocket Lawyer / Trust & Will:** Create wills, trusts, and power of attorney online.
- **VA.gov Survivors Benefits Page:** For dependents and family guidance.

Legacy Binder Prompts
- Will & Trust
- Life Insurance Policies
- Property Deeds
- VA Benefits Info
- Passwords & Key Contacts

Golden Nugget:
Don't just plan your legacy. Document it.

---

9. Ask Antwaun's Recommended Resource List

Financial Education YouTube Channels
- The Minority Mindset
- Graham Stephan
- Wealth Hacker – Jeff Rose
- Military Money Manual Podcast

Books to Keep on Your Shelf
- The Millionaire Next Door – Thomas Stanley
- I Will Teach You to Be Rich – Ramit Sethi
- Richest Man in Babylon – George Clason
- Set for Life – Scott Trench

Veteran Support Networks
- *Veterati* – Free mentorship for service members and spouses
- *AUSA (Association of the U.S. Army)* – Leadership and financial readiness programs

- *Military OneSource* – Free financial and legal counseling

Golden Nugget:
Don't just collect information; apply it. Knowledge without movement is wasted potential.

---

10. My Personal Resource Tracker

Use this space to log what you've tried, what's working, and what to explore next. Treat it like your ongoing mission log.

Area	Tool Used	Notes	Next Step
Budgeting	_____	_____	_____
Saving	_____	_____	_____
Investing	_____	_____	_____
Real Estate	_____	_____	_____
Insurance	_____	_____	_____
Education	_____	_____	_____

You don't need to master every tool on this list, just pick one category and start. Master it, automate it, then move on to the next. Remember: every great mission starts with preparation, execution, and persistence. You've got all three.

Your benefits are the blueprint. These tools are the weapons. Your mindset is the key.

About The Author

Antwaun Hill is a U.S. Army veteran, real estate professional, and founder of the Ask Antwaun brand, a movement dedicated to helping service members and veterans transform their military benefits into lifelong wealth.

Born in Miami, Florida and raised in Clayton County, Georgia, Antwaun enlisted in the U.S. Army in 2000, beginning a 13-year career that took him across the world through five permanent duty stations and two deployments. Rising to the rank of Chief Warrant Officer 2, he learned early that discipline, leadership, and adaptability weren't just military skills; they were wealth-building principles.

After transitioning from active duty, Antwaun continued serving his country as a civilian with the Department of Defense for another decade. But it wasn't until he discovered the power of real estate that his perspective on money and service truly shifted. He realized that while many service members worked tirelessly for their country, few were ever taught how to make their benefits work for them.

Today, as a licensed real estate agent in Hawaii, Antwaun has made it his mission to change that narrative. Through Ask Antwaun and the BAH Means Buy A House movement, he educates military families on leveraging their Basic Allowance for Housing (BAH), VA Loans, PCS moves, and Thrift Savings Plan (TSP) to create generational wealth. His approach combines financial literacy with practical, boots-on-the-ground strategy, empowering others to shift from surviving to thriving.

When he's not mentoring clients or speaking at military readiness events, Antwaun enjoys time with his family, exploring Hawaii's beaches, and continuing his own lifelong pursuit of growth. His motto is simple: You've already served your country; now it's time to make your money serve you.

Other books in this series

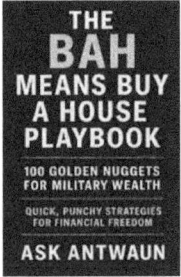